KU-330-024

My first book of telling the time

PRICE STERN SLOAN LIMITED, NORTHAMPTON, ENGLAND

The fun way to bring learning to life

This book is part of the **Questron** system, which offers children a unique aid to learning and endless hours of challenging entertainment.

The **Questron** Electronic Answer Wand uses a microchip to sense correct and incorrect answers with "right" or "wrong" sounds and lights. Victory sounds and lights reward the user when particular sets of questions or games are completed. Powered by a nine-volt alkaline battery, which is activated only when the wand is pressed on a page, **Questron** should have an exceptionally long life. The **Questron** Electronic Answer Wand can be used with any book in the **Questron** series.

A note to parents...

With **Questron**, right or wrong answers are indicated instantly and can be tried over and over again to reinforce learning and improve skills. Children need not be restricted to the books designated for their age group, as interests and rates of development vary widely. Also, within many of the books, certain pages are designed for the older end of the age group and will provide a stimulating challenge to younger children.

Many activities are designed at different levels. For example, the child can select an answer by recognizing a letter or by reading an entire word. The activities for pre-readers and early readers are intended to be used with parental assistance. Interaction with parents or older children will stimulate the learning experience.

Text and illustrations: copyright © 1986 Price/Stern/Sloan Publishers, Inc. Cover design: copyright © 1987 Price Stern Sloan Limited. All rights reserved under International and Pan-American Copyright Conventions. No part of this publication may be reproduced, stored in a retrieval system, or transmitted in any form or by any means, electronic, mechanical, photocopying, recording or otherwise, without the prior written permission of the publisher. Published in U.K. in 1987 by Price Stern Sloan Limited, John Clare House, The Avenue, Cliftonville, Northampton NN1 5BT.

Printed in Great Britain by
Purnell Book Production Limited
Member of the BPCC Group

How to start Questron®

Hold **Questron** at this angle and press the activator button firmly on the page.

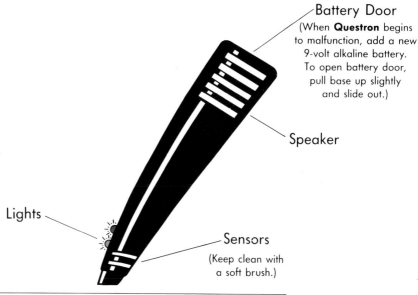

Battery Door
(When **Questron** begins to malfunction, add a new 9-volt alkaline battery. To open battery door, pull base up slightly and slide out.)

Speaker

Lights

Sensors
(Keep clean with a soft brush.)

How to use Questron®

Press
Press **Questron** firmly on the shape below, then lift it off.

Track
Press **Questron** down on "Start" and keep it pressed down as you move to "Finish".

Start

Finish

Right and wrong with Questron®

Press **Questron** on the square.

See the green light and hear the sound. This green light and sound say "You are correct".

Press **Questron** on the triangle.

The red light and sound say "Try again". Lift **Questron** off the page and wait for the sound to stop.

Press **Questron** on the circle.

Hear the victory sound. Don't be dazzled by the flashing lights. You deserve them.

Good Day

Press **Questron** on the word that correctly completes each sentence.

The beginning of the day is called

| lunchtime. | morning. | evening. |

The middle of the day is called

| morning. | afternoon. | noon. |

When it gets dark outside we say it is

| night. | dawn. | Saturday. |

When we want to know exactly
what time it is we look at a

| thermometer. | clock. | radio. |

Clocks measure

| time. | distance. | pounds. |

Each day has 24

| months. | weeks. | hours. |

Good Times

There are many different kinds of clocks.
Press **Questron** on the picture that matches each clock name.

Alarm clock

Digital clock

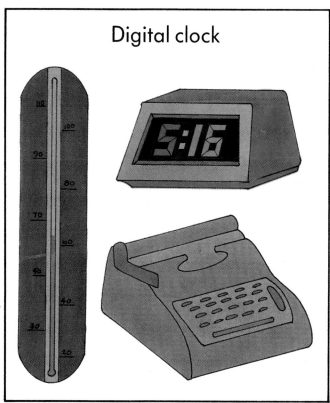

Grandfather clock

Wristwatch

Familiar Faces

Press **Questron** on the correct answer.

A clock measures

| time. | weight. | temperature. |

The front of the clock is called the

| head. | window. | face. |

There are   10   12   14   numbers on these clocks.

Which clock face is correct?

A Show of Hands

Press **Questron** on the answer that correctly completes each sentence.

The pointers on a clock are called

ears.	arms.	hands.

On clocks with hands, the hands are always

the same length.	different colours.	different lengths.

One hand is always

longer.	curved.	square.

The other hand is always

rounder.	shorter.	wavy.

Some clocks have 3 hands.
The third hand is always

much fatter.	much thinner.	the same size.

The third hand always moves

much faster.	much slower.	the same speed.

As Easy as 1, 2, 3

Press **Questron** on the word that
correctly completes each sentence.

The red hand measures

doughnuts.	hours.	minutes.

The green hand measures

minutes.	rainfall.	hours.

The black hand measures

minutes.	inches.	seconds.

The red hand is called the

minute hand.	left hand.	hour hand.

The green hand is called the

hour hand.	minute hand.	right hand.

The black hand is called the

second hand.	third hand.	thin hand.

Look! No Hands!

Press **Questron** on the word that correctly completes each sentence.

This kind of clock has no hands at all. This is a

numerical clock.	digital clock.	grandfather clock.

These numbers measure

hours.	minutes.	days.

These numbers measure

months.	minutes.	hours.

Digital clocks have no

hands.	numbers.	alarms.

Some digital clocks have smaller numbers that measure

minutes.	seconds.	electricity.

Hour Town

The hour hand takes one hour to move from one number to the next. Look at the clocks in each picture. Track **Questron** on the answer that shows the number of hours that have passed. Start on the ☆.

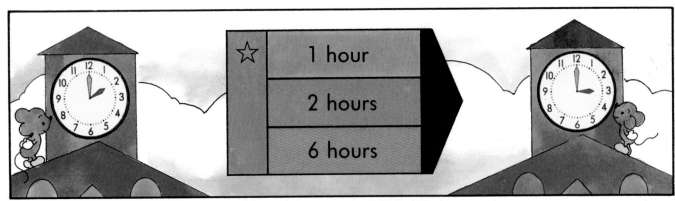

☆ | 1 hour
2 hours
6 hours

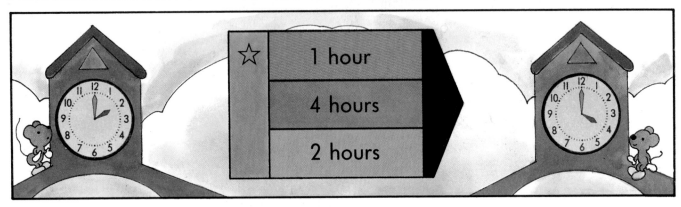

☆ | 1 hour
4 hours
2 hours

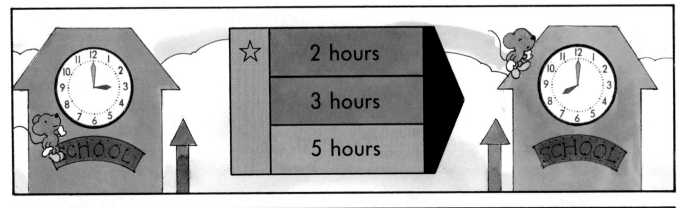

☆ | 2 hours
3 hours
5 hours

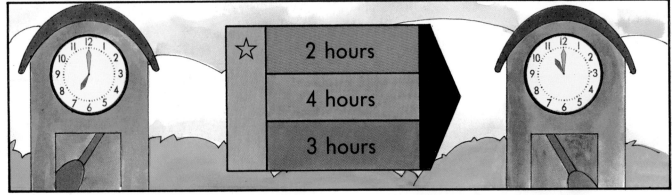

☆ | 2 hours
4 hours
3 hours

Starting at 12, how many hours will it take for the hour hand to go all the way around to the 12 again?

10 hours   11 hours   12 hours

Minute Man

It takes 5 minutes for the minute hand to move from one number to the next. Look at the clocks in each picture. Track **Questron** on the answer that shows how many minutes have passed. Start on the ☆.

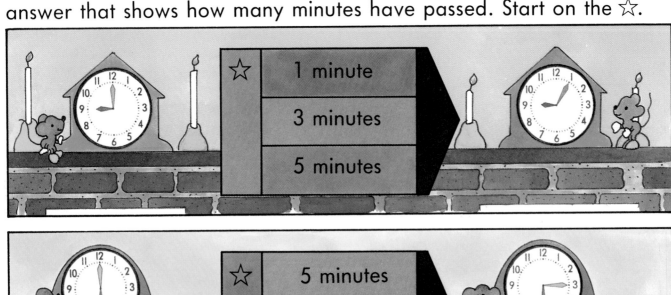

☆ | 1 minute
3 minutes
5 minutes

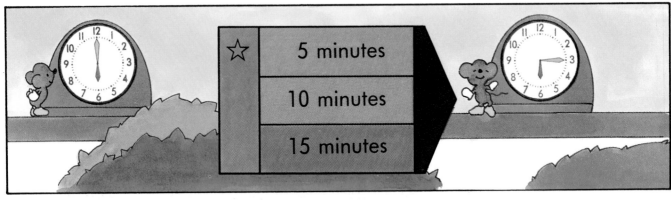

☆ | 5 minutes
10 minutes
15 minutes

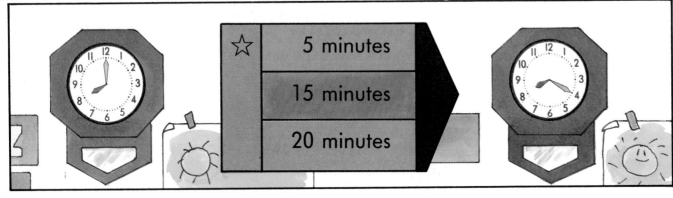

☆ | 5 minutes
15 minutes
20 minutes

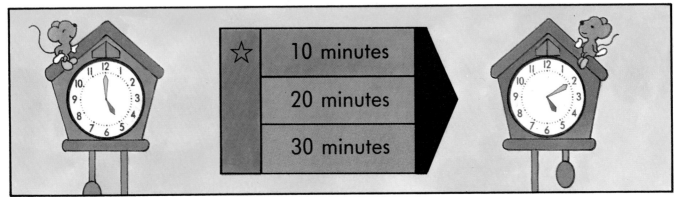

☆ | 10 minutes
20 minutes
30 minutes

Press **Questron** on the correct answers.

Starting at 12, how many minutes will it take for the minute hand to go all the way around to the 12 again?

12 minutes	30 minutes	60 minutes

The minute hand moves

slower	the same speed	faster

than the hour hand.

There are

30	60	120

minutes in one hour.

How many times will the minute hand go around the clock in 1 hour?

1 time	2 times	12 times

Just a Second!

It takes 5 seconds for the second hand to move from one number to the next. Look at the clocks in each picture. Track **Questron** on the answer that shows how many seconds have passed. Start on the ☆.

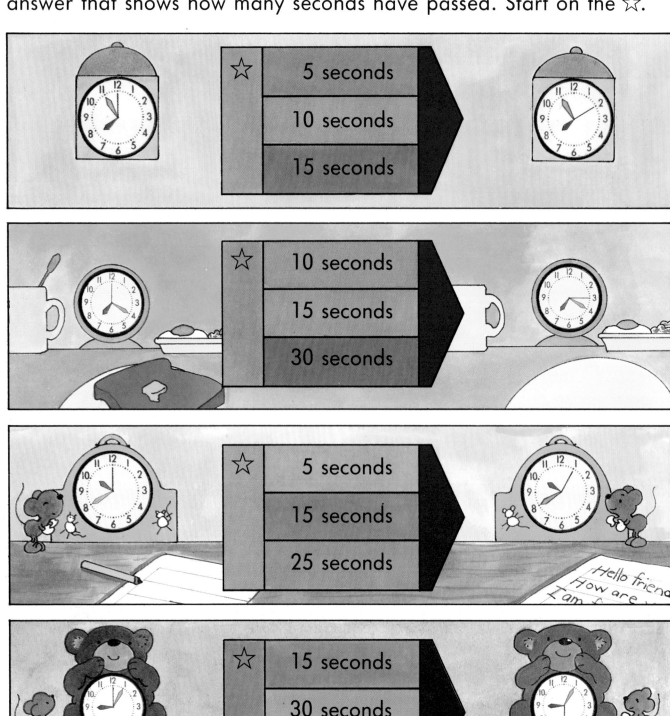

☆ 5 seconds
10 seconds
15 seconds

☆ 10 seconds
15 seconds
30 seconds

☆ 5 seconds
15 seconds
25 seconds

☆ 15 seconds
30 seconds
45 seconds

Press **Questron** on the correct answers.

Starting at 12, how many seconds will it take for the
second hand to go all the way around to the 12 again?

12 seconds	60 seconds	100 seconds

The second hand moves

faster	the same speed.	slower

than the minute hand.

There are

60 seconds	10 seconds	5 seconds

in a minute.

How many minutes does it take for the
second hand to go around one time?

1 minute	5 minutes	60 minutes

Racing the Clock

The race starts at 12. Look at the clocks at the end of the race.
How long does it take each runner to reach the finishing line?
Track **Questron** through each lane to the correct answer. Start on the ☆.

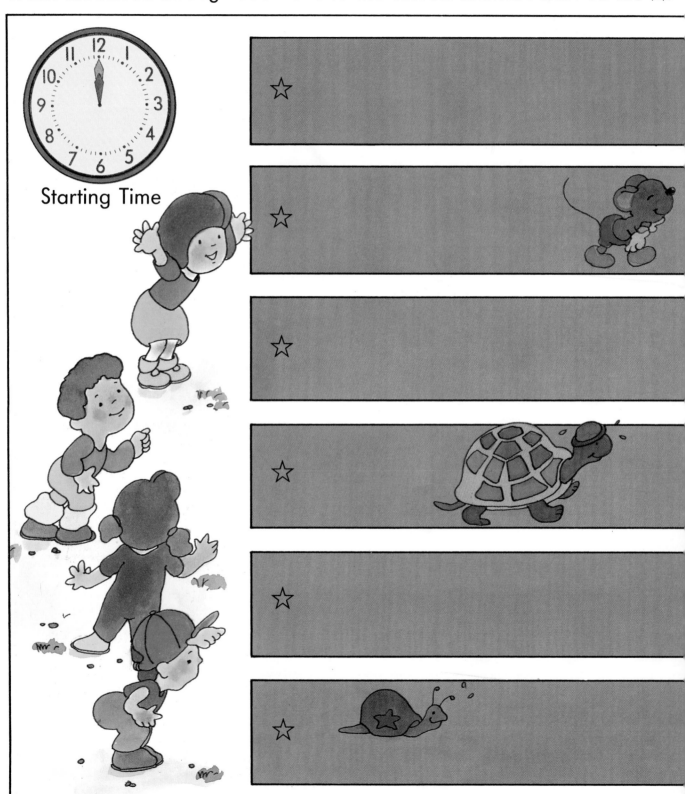

Starting Time

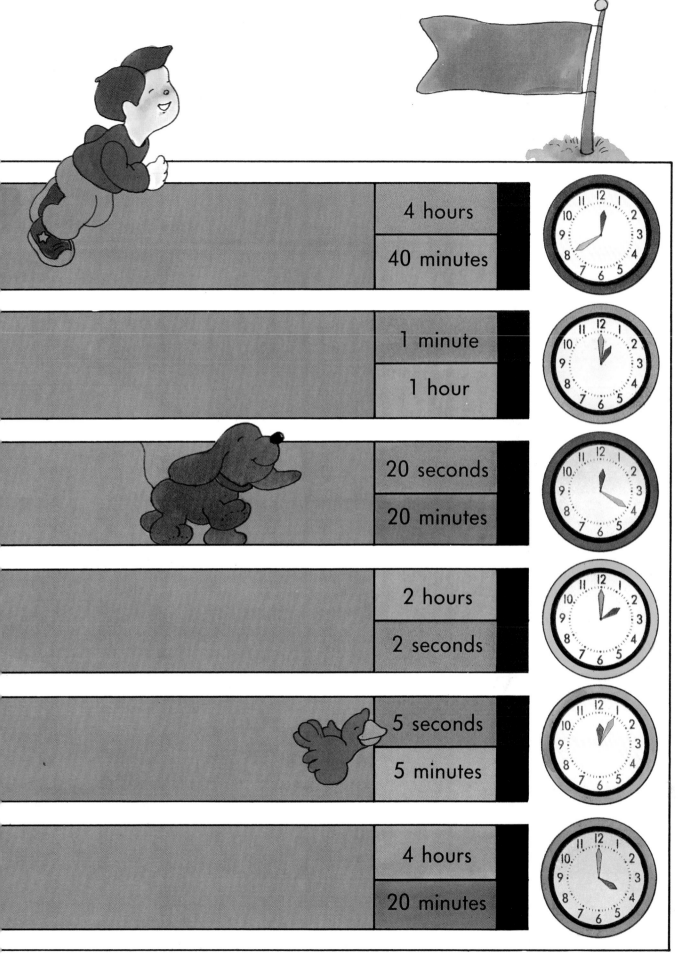

4 hours

40 minutes

1 minute

1 hour

20 seconds

20 minutes

2 hours

2 seconds

5 seconds

5 minutes

4 hours

20 minutes

Time for Repairs

Mr. Fixit has repaired these clocks, but they all stopped running soon after being started. Each clock started with all three hands pointing to the 12. How many hours, minutes and seconds did each clock run before it stopped? Press **Questron** on the answer that shows how long each clock ran before it stopped.

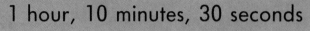

1 hour, 10 minutes, 30 seconds

1 hour, 10 minutes, 45 seconds

1 hour, 15 minutes, 30 seconds

8 hours, 10 minutes, 30 seconds

8 hours, 30 minutes, 10 seconds

10 hours, 8 minutes, 10 seconds

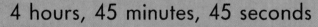

4 hours, 45 minutes, 45 seconds

6 hours, 45 minutes, 45 seconds

4 hours, 15 minutes, 45 seconds

Mr. Fixit didn't have any better luck repairing these digital clocks. Each clock started at 12, but all the clocks stopped later that day. How many hours, minutes, and seconds did each clock run before it stopped? Press **Questron** on the answer that shows how long each clock ran before it stopped.

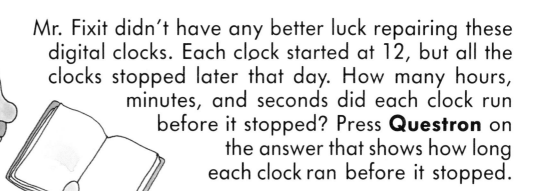

2 hours, 30 minutes, 15 seconds

3 hours, 30 minutes, 15 seconds

3 hours, 20 minutes, 15 seconds

6 hours, 5 minutes, 30 seconds

9 hours, 5 minutes, 30 seconds

6 hours, 30 minutes, 5 seconds

10 hours, 10 minutes, 15 seconds

10 hours, 15 minutes, 10 seconds

11 hours, 10 minutes, 15 seconds

On the Hour

When the hour hand is on the 5 and the minute hand is on the 12, we say it is 5 o'clock. What time is it in each of these pictures? Press **Questron** on the correct time for each picture.

12 o'clock
8 o'clock
7 o'clock

3 o'clock
6 o'clock
9 o'clock

10 o'clock
9 o'clock
6 o'clock

11 o'clock
5 o'clock
3 o'clock

7 o'clock	
10 o'clock	
12 o'clock	

5 o'clock	
1 o'clock	
3 o'clock	

4 o'clock	
2 o'clock	
7 o'clock	

5 o'clock	
3 o'clock	
7 o'clock	

It's About Time

When the minute hand is between the 6 and the 12, it is before the hour. This clock shows that it is 10 minutes before 3 o'clock. We say it is "10 minutes to 3 o'clock" or just "10 to 3." Press **Questron** on the correct time for each clock.

When the minute hand is between the 12 and the 6, we say that it is past the hour. This clock shows that it is 20 minutes past 2 o'clock. We say it is "20 past 2." We can also say that it is "two-twenty." Press **Questron** on the correct time for each clock.

Half-Time Show

This clock shows that it is three-thirty. The minute hand is → halfway around the clock, so we say it is "half past three."

 When the minute hand is on the 3, we say that it is "quarter past the hour." When the minute hand is on the 9, we say that it is "quarter to the hour." →

Press **Questron** on the correct time for each clock.

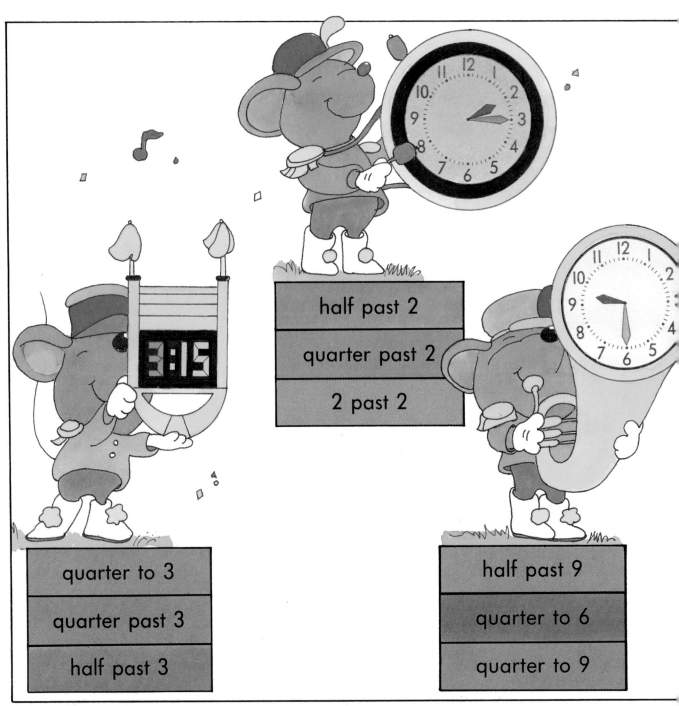

half past 2

quarter past 2

2 past 2

quarter to 3

quarter past 3

half past 3

half past 9

quarter to 6

quarter to 9

quarter to 4

quarter past 9

half past 4

half past 6

half past 7

half past 12

quarter past 7

half past 3

quarter to 7

quarter past 6

quarter to 6

half past 9

Night and Day

When the clock shows 12 o'clock and it is dark outside, it is midnight.
When it is 12 o'clock in the daytime, it is midday or noon.
Press **Questron** on the picture that shows the correct time of day.

12 noon

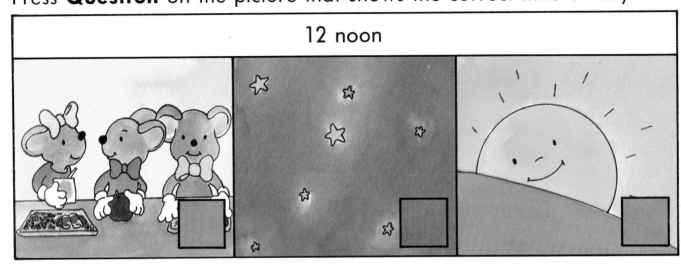

12 midnight

10 to 12 midday

quarter past midnight

5 past 12 midday

20 to midnight

Twice a Day

A day is 24 hours long. There are only 12 hours on a clock so the hour hand must go round twice each day. The time between midnight and noon is called A.M. The time between noon and midnight is called P.M. Press **Questron** on the picture that matches the time.

3:30 A.M.

2:00 P.M.

7:30 A.M.

6:15 A.M.

8:00 P.M.

12:15 P.M.

12:45 P.M.

8:00 A.M.

1:00 P.M.

Don't Be Late

Morning is the time between midnight and noon.
Afternoon is the time between noon and when it starts
to get dark. If it is the first part of the day we say
it is early in the day. If it is the last part of the day we
say it is late in the day.
Press **Questron** on the correct answer.

What do we call the first part of the afternoon?

| early afternoon | mid-afternoon | late afternoon |

What part of the morning is called the late morning?

| the first part | the middle part | the last part |

When you wake up on a school day, it is

| early morning. | late morning. | early afternoon. |

When you eat lunch, it is

| early morning. | early afternoon. | late afternoon. |

When the sun comes up, it is

| early afternoon. | late morning. | early morning. |

When it just starts to get dark, it is

| late morning. | early afternoon. | late afternoon. |

Good Night

The time between when the sun goes down and when it gets completely dark outside is called evening.
Press **Questron** on the correct answer for each picture.

early morning
12 midnight
2:35 P.M.

1:00 A.M.
1:00 P.M.
11:00 P.M.

2:00 P.M.
evening
half past 12

"good morning"
"good day"
"good night"

Another exciting children's series
Look, listen and join in the fun with

The Wee Sing range of cassettes and activity books are compiled by experienced preschool and early school teachers. The tapes include songs, games and rhymes. The books have the musical notes of the melody lines, so that children can have fun, sing along – and learn, too!

The Wee Sing and Colour series adds yet another dimension. The books not only contain the complete lyrics of the songs and rhymes – they also have line drawings of favourite characters to colour.

Wee Sing provides an hour of entertainment and music, and a songbook with no less than 64 pages. **Wee Sing and Colour** gives you some 30 minutes of songs, games and rhymes and a 48-page colouring book.

Wee Sing – early learning made fun.

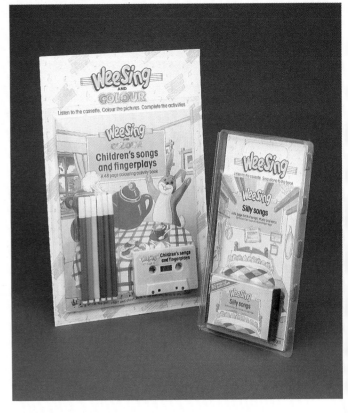

Wee Sing

**Children's songs and fingerplays
Rhymes for play
Nursery rhymes and lullabies
Silly songs**

Wee Sing & Colour

**Children's songs and fingerplays
Musical games and rhymes
Christmas songs**

See what Questron has to say

Approximately how many minutes does each Wee Sing tape last?

How many pages of activity and fun does each Wee Sing and Colour book provide?

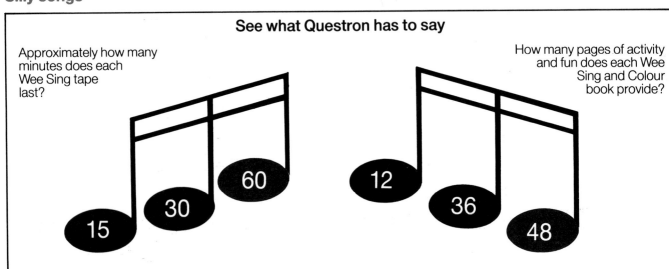

Another new product range from PSS – if you have difficulty in obtaining Wee Sing from your local stockist, please contact Price Stern Sloan Limited, John Clare House, The Avenue, Northampton NN1 5BT. Telephone (0604) 230344.